Creative
Candlescaping

Creative Candlescaping

Terry Taylor

LARK BOOKS

A Division of Sterling Publishing Company, Inc.

NEW YORK

ART DIRECTOR
Susan McBride

PRINCIPAL PHOTOGRAPHY
Keith Wright

ASSISTANT ART DIRECTOR
Hannes Charen

COVER DESIGN
Barbara Zaretsky

PRODUCTION ASSISTANCE
Shannon Yokeley

EDITORIAL ASSISTANCE
Delores Gosnell
Veronika Alice Gunter
Rain Newcomb

ART INTERN
Lorelei Buckley

SPECIAL PHOTOGRAPHY
Sanoma Syndication:
Dennis Brandsma, 58;
Freek Esser, 68; Rene
Gonkel, 5; Peter Kooijman,
13, 14, 91; Eric van Lokven,
12, 61; Thomas Pelgrom, 51;
Dolf Straatemeier, 53, 80,
92; George v.d. Wijngaard,
55, 77; Hans Zeegers, 15, 52

Library of Congress Cataloging-in-Publication Data Available

10 9 8 7 6 5 4 3 2 1

First Edition

Published by Lark Books, a division of
Sterling Publishing Co., Inc.
387 Park Avenue South, New York, N.Y. 10016

Distributed in Canada by Sterling Publishing,
c/o Canadian Manda Group, One Atlantic Ave., Suite 105
Toronto, Ontario, Canada M6K 3E7

Distributed in the U.K. by:
Guild of Master Craftsman Publications Ltd.
Castle Place
166 High Street
Lewes
East Sussex
England
BN7 1XU
Tel: (+ 44) 1273 477374
Fax: (+ 44) 1273 478606
Email: pubs@thegmcgroup.com
Web: www.gmcpublications.com

Distributed in Australia by Capricorn Link (Australia) Pty Ltd., P.O. Box 704, Windsor,
NSW 2756 Australia

If you have questions or comments about this book, please contact:
Lark Books
67 Broadway
Asheville, NC 28801
(828) 253-0467

Printed in China

ISBN 1-57990-406-8

Contents

Introduction

The best sitting room at Manor Farm was a good, long, dark-panelled room. . . . In all sorts of recesses, and on all kinds of brackets, stood massive old silver candle-sticks with four branches each. The carpet was up, the candles burnt bright, the fire blazed and crackled on the hearth, and merry voices and light-hearted laughter rang through the room.

The Pickwick Papers,
Charles Dickens

Perhaps, in one of your daytime reveries, you long for a warm and overstuffed, chintz-patterned sitting room filled with silver candlesticks, porcelain, and—why not?—a butler at your beck and call. We all long for some escape from the reality (and lights) of our modern world: the bluish glow of computer screens, the flicker of television sets, and the harsh fluorescent lighting of shopping places.

Not many of us have (or want) a "best" sitting room or "massive" silver candlesticks, but a softly flickering candle, accompanying the sound of pleasant conversation, music, or just peace and quiet (take your pick), is high on most everyone's want list at the end of a long day.

Candles shouldn't be saved solely for special occasions or when the electricity is on the fritz. Candles are for everyday use, whether you light them or not. Make a take-out supper for two a memorable end-of-the-day surprise with a single

Use this book as a helpful and inspiring guide to using candles indoors and out, for everyday use or for festive celebrations. Remember, this is just a guide. Your personal tastes and desires are to be trusted above all. And who knows, perhaps you'll find a use for that little red wagon the kids have outgrown, after all.

lit candle. Use candles to create a five-alarm celebration to impress any birthday boy (or girl), no matter what his or her age. Pamper your guests (or yourself) with a combination of candlelight and flowers. Change the look of a room in a snap, simply by mixing colorful candles with things you have around the house. Soothe ragged nerves with softly scented candles while you take a long, hot bath.

There's no excuse for not having candles at hand. Candles are everywhere: in home decor and home improvement stores, craft and discount stores, even on the shelves of your local grocery store. Scented or unscented. Plain or fanciful. Beeswax, paraffin, and even soy! In any color, shape, and size you might need or desire. There's no reason for using plain white plumber's candles, unless your personal tastes lean toward white, unscented candles.
And who can fault that?

Candle Basics

Name That Candle

When you shop for candles, it's easy to become bewildered by the overwhelming variety of available shapes and sizes. Let's not worry about color, scent, or type of wax used; those are other matters altogether. By asking yourself a few simple questions you'll be able to decide which type of candle to purchase.

Is the candle simply for display or will you light it? Do you have a candleholder at home or will you need to purchase or create one? Once you answer those questions, you're almost ready to purchase a candle. A working vocabulary of candle styles may help you sort things out.

Tapers are tall, slim candles, generally wider at the bottom and narrowing toward the tip; they require a candleholder for support. Tapers can be as tiny as the 2-inch-tall (5 cm) candles used on top of a birthday cake, to 18-inch-tall (46 cm) altar candles.

Votive or vigil candles, as they are sometimes called, are generally 2 inches (5 cm) tall and about 1 1/2 inches (3.8 cm) wide. They are meant to be placed in containers, usually small glass ones, which contain the melted wax.

Tea lights are tiny candles, not unlike votives, that are fitted into disposable metal cups. In general they are 1 1/2 inches (3.8 cm) in diameter and a scant 3/4 inch (1.9 cm) tall.

Just as their name implies, pillar candles are rigid, freestanding candles, designed to be used on a nonflammable, flat surface. They may be cylindrical, square, rectangular, or oval; smooth-sided, grooved, decorated, or textured. Large and multi-wick pillars are less likely to drip wax. Be careful to always use some sort of protection underneath a pillar; dyes in the wax of some pillars may stain surfaces.

Container candles are made with a low-melting-point paraffin. Melted wax is poured into any type of container, from translucent glass tumblers to artfully rusted metal containers; from antique, porcelain tea cups to terra cotta garden pots.

Discontinue use of a container candle when $1/2$ inch (1.3 cm) of wax remains. If you're particularly fond of the container, set it in hot water to loosen and remove the wax (see page 11). You can replace the wax with a votive candle or make your own container candle.

Save colorfully printed tins from Asian food markets or the ethnic foods aisle of your grocery store to create a special arrangement of container candles. If tin cans don't appeal to you, use containers made of glass, china, terra cotta, and those seashells you gathered on your last trip to the beach. You'll need to wash and dry each container before you use it.

Purchase paraffin, candle dye, and tabbed candle wicks at your local craft store. Melt the wax in a double boiler or in a pan you will set aside just for melting wax. Color the wax, if you wish, with a small amount of dye. Place the tabbed wick in your mold and carefully pour in the melted wax. If you're an absolute novice, check your local library for a book on candlemaking.

Candleholders

When choosing a candleholder, keep in mind the type of candle you have chosen as well as the overall look you want to achieve. Hand-dipped beeswax tapers can look elegantly formal in traditional silver candlesticks and rustically casual in hand-thrown pottery ware. You can display pillar candles on china platters, slices of stone, ceramic tiles, or even in toy wagons (page 25). Tea cups, colorful glassware, and even sand-filled cloth bags (92) can be used to hold tea lights.

Metal is a common and ideal material for a candlestick: it doesn't burn! The sparkle of glass candleholders softly reflects and refracts the glow of candlelight. As long as the candle flame doesn't come in too close contact with the container, even paper bags can be put into use as candleholders.

Inventory your living spaces for possibilities: kitchen cabinets, kids rooms, storeroom or garage. They'll probably yield candleholders just waiting to be discovered. Take those rarely used glass goblets from the top shelf of the cabinet and fill them with glass jewels and votives (page 40); or give a toy fire engine a five-alarm load of votives to carry (page 50).

Once you start looking with an open mind, you'll find candleholders everywhere.

Almost any object can hold a candle, but there are three common-sense rules you should follow when making a selection.

Rule 1: The candleholder must hold the candle securely upright in or on a nonflammable surface. Candleholders for tapers should have a hole or a sharp pricket to hold the candle.

Rule 2: A candleholder should protect surfaces from dripping wax.

Rule 3: The candle should never overpower the holder or look top heavy. It's visually unpleasant, and the sight of a falling, lit candle could induce a panic attack, to say the least.

Aside from those rules, anything goes.

*If you dream of five candles,
your future will be filled with
happiness and prosperity.*

CLEANING
Candleholders

Why clean up candleholders? Well, for one, you might want to display that branched candelabra with the rest of grandmother's silver in the breakfront, and it wouldn't do to have its lustrous surface encrusted with wax, now would it? For another, the waxy traces of the bright red candle might spoil the look of your new lavender tapers. Follow the simple directions below to clean your candleholders.

To clean wax out of a votive cup or to remove the remnants of a spent container candle, soak the candleholder in hot, soapy water for 30 minutes. Remove any large portions of wax, then scrub with a cloth to remove the rest of the wax.

If your candleholder has curves or deep crevices, put it in the freezer for 30 minutes. Use a blunt instrument, such as a wooden skewer or toothpick, to easily peel off the wax. If needed, soak the holder in warm, soapy water and wipe it with a cloth to remove the last traces of wax.

Floating candles require more than just a container:
They need water! Fashion your own sea of serenity for
the living room or dining table. Float petals and small
flowers, or lightweight, blown-glass bubbles along with
your candles.

A clear, glass flower frog placed inside a vase or bowl is
a clever and practical way to array a bright bouquet of
ultra-thin tapers.

Color

There's nothing more personal than choosing a color. It's the choice that most closely expresses the self you present to the world. At heart, are you a brightly hued extrovert, an earth-toned realist, or the thinker who prefers calming shades of grey? Choose the colors that speak to you; there are no hard and fast rules for using color.

Mixing colors—copper, silver, and white—is contemporary and stylish. This arrangement of unlit pillar and globe candles functions as an architectural statement on the mantelpiece. For special occasions, use lighted votives or tea lights to highlight the colors and shape of an arrangement without sacrificing all of the candles.

Burn a white candle for luck and happiness in your new home.

The matte white of the candleholders and topiary containers looks both casual and elegant at the same time. The white flatters and contrasts the muted green foliage. You may not have a conservatory, but the principle remains the same: You can't go wrong using white candles.

Fussy candle arrangements can (and do) get in the way of stimulating conversation or romantic banter at the dinner table. Slender, gentle-hued tapers in simple glass holders create a centerpiece that is visually pleasing and not-at-all distracting.

These simple shapes are made more interesting by variegated layers of icy blue. The peaceful colors nicely contrast with the dark granite surface and accents of golden ginkgo leaves.

16

Sleek geometry and intriguing textural surfaces create a bold statement when placed against the vibrant color of the walls. The arrangement is grounded with an understated black tray and reflected in the mirrored surface.

A single row of cactus-colored votive candles on this windowsill echoes the vibrant color of the room. Square glass candleholders accent the clean architectural lines of the long window.

Modern, Asian flair best describes this arrangement. The strong indigo patterns of the porcelain orbs are echoed in the blue of the candles. A small tatami mat unifies the contrasting shapes. The understated lines of the black steel candleholder complement the display.

The Language of CANDLE COLORS

The ritual of burning candles for religious ceremonies or magical rites is as old as history. Throughout recorded history candles have been burned as a part of celebrations, as an act of atonement, and to evoke supplication.

In 1942 the folklore researcher Henri Gamache wrote an intriguing pamphlet entitled *The Master Book of Candle Burning or How to Burn Candles for Every Purpose.* He examined the rituals of candle burning to draw luck, love, or money, and to protect against the evil eye. Candles of different colors are used to evoke varying effects. It's no accident that many of the powers assigned to candle colors reflect qualities also associated with those colors in everyday life.

Red: strength, courage, power, love, and passion

Orange: luck, energy, change of plans, and attraction

Yellow: inspiration, imagination, devotion, and endurance

Green: growth, abundance, money, luck, and faith

Blue: healing, relaxation, contemplation, and wisdom

Purple: royalty, spirituality, devotion, and vision

Violet: expansion, trust, and innocence

White: purity, healing, and rest

Lavender: compassion and inspiration

Pink: love, joy, and friendship

White: purity, protection, and direction

Brown: grounding, good fortune, wealth

Black: sorrow, elegance, and sophistication

Silver: intuition, sensitivity, and creativity

Gold: good fortune and blessingz

Choose your candle color wisely!

Waxes

Until the discovery of paraffin wax in the 1850s, candles were usually made in the home from natural waxes and rendered animal fats. Paraffin and beeswax are the most common, but not the only, waxes used for making candles today.

Paraffin is an odorless and semitransparent hard wax. It's easily colored by dyes and, because it's odorless, an ideal wax for scenting. Natural beeswax has a golden color and a sweet fragrance. Soy wax—new to the candle market—is manufactured from soybeans. Transparent gel candles are made from a mineral oil gelled with a copolymer.

A dream with a red candle in it illuminates your hidden passions and desires.

Scent and Aromatherapy

Scented or unscented? Like a color choice, it's up to you. Using scent to effect the mind and emotions—aromatherapy—is a time-honored practice that has become more popular in recent years. The scented, essential oils from flowers, herbs, spices, and other natural materials are extracted by distillation. The oils are used alone or in a variety of products including candles, which are available in a wide spectrum of scents, from old standbys like lavender and citronella to exotic ylang-ylang and green tea. Aromatherapy practitioners suggest using different scents for different effects.

Rosemary: invigorates

Citronella: repels insects

Jasmine: alleviates depression

Ylang-ylang: soothes anxiety

Vetiver: eases insomnia

Lavender: stimulates

Valeria: soothes

Bear in mind that many people are acutely sensitive to scent. If you appreciate scented candles, by all means enjoy them. One caveat: Never burn scented candles at the dinner table. The scent will conflict with the aroma of the food and possibly confound your sense of taste.

19

The Candle Indoors

Playing with Light

Most of the day we're trapped in the harsh light of the workplace or illuminated by the steady, bluish glow of the computer screen. In the evening, a bit of flickering light (and we don't mean the flicker of the television screen) is the perfect antidote to the daytime routine.

Playing with light is one of the chief pleasures of using candles in our homes. You know the old saying: Like a moth to a flame.

Glass candleholders—colored, faceted, and crystal cut—refract light in beautiful ways. Combine that effect with a mirrored tabletop or by placing the candle in front of a hanging mirror—let the magic play of light begin.

Small candles placed behind an openwork grill create an interesting contrast between the flicker of the flames and the solidity of the rusted steel.

When a candle burns blue, there will be a frost.

Candle SAFETY

Candle safety is based on common sense, but it never hurts to restate these obvious precautions.

Never leave a burning candle unattended.

Never place a burning candle near something that can catch fire.

Keep burning candles out of the reach of toddlers and the wagging tails of man's best friend.

Don't burn candles for more than four hours at a time.

Moving a lighted candle is never a good idea. Extinguish a candle before you move it from one place to another (unless, of course, the power is out and you have to navigate up dark stairs to an even darker hallway).

A pea-size portion of non-hardening candle adhesive on a taper's base will prevent your candle from toppling over onto something flammable.

Summon the delicate tracery of Victorian ironwork, a shadowy feast for the eyes. The Victorians amused themselves with parlor shadow games and created vignettes behind backlit scrims. Use a richly colored oriental rug as a table cover and arrange a baker's dozen of candles in cast-off bird cages. Light the candles and gaze at the shifting shadows projected on the walls and ceiling. Her Majesty would no doubt approve.

Using What You Have

There's no need to rush out and purchase candleholders—unless you have the burning desire to shop. Few homes don't have at least one candleholder, if not several, stashed in closets or lying in wait in the garage. Plus, it's easy and fun to transform an object you have on hand into an unexpected candleholder.

Whatever you do, don't upset this little red wagon. You can roll your candlelight to wherever you need it. Just keep it out of your toddler's way. Wouldn't a toy wheelbarrow make a delightful candleholder for the garden?

Beaded candle shades and votive holders are decorative accessories that create romantic effects. Use a beaded basket for an unexpected take on this popular trend. The circular form of the basket throws a twinkling mandala of light around it. Be sure you line the bottom of the basket with foil to protect it from wax drips.

Brass candlesticks accumulate, whether they're gifts from friends or impulsive yard sale purchases. More than likely, you can lay your hands on two or three right away. They don't need to match to become a classic candle display—simple white tapers unify the different styles.

Let's be frank: You have a collection if you have more than three of anything (children and pets don't count). What better way to showcase your collection than to use it? The sheer number of candlesticks used in this arrangement says, "This is a special occasion."

Need a new look for unadorned votive holders (or small jars) that's easy to execute? And it uses only two materials that you probably have on hand: simple bamboo place mats are wrapped around the glass containers and secured with raffia, twine, wire, or even long strands of grass from the garden. What could be easier to do and result in such a sophisticated look?

Place a fancifully shaped plate filled with tiny globe candles in an unexpected place. Set it on a stack of rustic stools with a single, large pinecone nearby, and enjoy the beautiful display of light, texture, and color.

Polished rocks provide a fireproof nest in this contemporary squared bowl. The simplicity of the arrangement complements the clean lines of the tabletop.

When a candle burns
with a tall, straight flame,
listen for the knock of
a stranger at your door.

The luminous beauty of
this orb literally comes from
within: tiny metal cups in
the hollow interior hold tea
lights. A candle-powered
chandelier of this scale and
design is not really practical,
but with something this
fabulous, who cares about
practicality!

A tall glass vase doesn't have to hold flowers. Use it
as a striking hurricane shade for a solitary pillar candle.
Arrange some dried or fresh natural materials around
the base or let it stand alone. Several vases massed
together make a striking display (page 78).

The large beeswax church candles, tin candleholders, *milagros*, and the *santos* are travel souvenirs from Mexico. Mementos and collectibles can become distinctive elements for candlescaping. Tuck votives amid your collection of snow globes from every state, give your collection of cobalt blue glassware nighttime illumination with tea lights, or arrange your favorite lanterns outdoors (page 72).

Some candles, like this beautifully detailed beeswax taper, should never be lit. The baroque flowers on the tapers are an amusing contrast to the folk-art tin appliqués on the candlestick.

Candle CARE

The curving arch of the candleholder brings together the differing shapes of the chunky candles and the smooth stone balls.

When a candle sparks, the person opposite it will receive a letter.

Store tapers flat to prevent warping. Place them in a cool, dark, and dry place, away from a heat source.

Candle colors and any decorative trim fade when left in strong light for an extended period of time. Don't expose them to direct sunlight or indoor spotlights.

Keep matches, wick trimmings, and foreign objects out of the candle wax. Not only are they unsightly, they can catch fire.

Trim wicks to ¼ inch (6 mm) prior to each use. A trimmed wick burns more evenly than a partially burned one and is less likely to sputter or send an overflow of hot wax unexpectedly down the side of the candle.

A lightly abrasive fabric—nylon net, chiffon, or even pantyhose—removes dust and dirt from candle surfaces. Test clean a small area with gentle pressure before you vigorously attack the dust.

If a candle's wick becomes too short to light, use a sharp knife to carve away enough wax to expose fresh wick. Then trim ¼ inch (6 mm) of wax off the top of the candle and burn the candle to reshape its appearance.

35

These silvery, fluted candleholders come from humble beginnings: They're tartlet molds from a kitchen store. (You also could use vintage gelatin molds.) You'll need an inexpensive rivet tool from the home improvement store, an awl, file, and a small block of scrap wood to make the holders.

Place a mold on the scrap wood. Use the awl to pierce a tiny hole centered on the bottom of each one. Carefully enlarge the hole with the awl until you can slip a rivet into its hole. File the rough edge of metal on the bottom of each mold. Align two molds, back to back, and rivet them together.

A rustic twig bench is a charming holder for a rectangular, multi-wick candle. Tapers or votives might present a fire hazard, but this type of candle is less likely to spill melted wax. Tuck a bit of reindeer moss around the bottom of the candle to disguise the foil placed underneath it.

Not Your Usual Candlesticks

Using what you have is a fine dictum to follow. Using what you have in an unusual way is an even better suggestion. Why not put that little used bowling ball to good use with tapers?

Crisp, fresh apples can be fashioned quickly into delightful, if temporary, candleholders. You'll need a corer, a sharp paring knife, and a little lemon juice. Select the firmest apples you can find, such as the bright green Granny Smith, the golden Gala stippled with red, or the dark crimson Red Delicious. Make an initial circular cut in the stem end of the apple with the corer. Use the paring knife to enlarge the diameter of the cut. A shallow cut will accommodate a tea light; a deeper cut will hold a votive. Squeeze a little lemon juice on the cut surface to slow the inevitable browning of the flesh.

Turnips are harder to hollow out than apples, but the technique you use is almost the same. Create an initial cut with a corer, then use a small spoon to slowly scoop out the flesh until there's only a shell remaining. Create tripod candleholders with large nails tied together with twine or raffia. Votives or tea lights will provide just the right golden glow for these tiny turnip lanterns.

A saw, hammer, and a few nails are all you need to create this candle lineup. Gather some sturdy, fallen branches (or save limbs from judicious tree pruning), saw them into different lengths, and drive a nail into each one to serve as a pricket. Alternate candles and fruits in your lineup, or use different sizes and contrasting colors of candles.

Turn a simple take-out supper into a special event. Reclaim those rarely used goblets: fill them with richly colored glass marbles (or river rocks, tiny seashells, or sand), then nestle a small votive or tea light in each one.

For festive affairs in late summer, create candle-holders for thin tapers with a colorful variety of shapely bell peppers. You also can use crisp, red apples in the fall or bright oranges in late winter.

Arrange the peppers upright on a platter. Use a very sharp, pointed knife to pierce small holes in the tops of the peppers. Start with a very small hole, enlarging it as needed to accommodate the taper. Use an apple corer to make larger holes for tapers in solid fruits and vegetables.

Hugs and kisses? Or game pieces for a weighty (and unwieldy) game of
tic-tac-toe? At first glance, you'd be hard pressed to identify these concrete objects
as candleholders. But when you're looking for candleholders, everything deserves a
second look. A striking garden sculpture, nestled in smooth pebbles or grass, this
piece also could light the way up to the back deck.

Building-supply products aren't strictly utilitarian anymore—some are finding a second life as chic decorating accessories. Post supports, fence caps, and galvanized pipe fittings can be made into innovative candleholders.

These wooden candleholders were created from finials, newel posts, and deck rails found in the local home improvement store. Fencing finials become candleholders with a small nail driven in the top to create a pricket for the candle (that's the sharp, pointy thing on some candlesticks). In their purchased state, newel posts and deck rails may be too tall for the tabletop. A handsaw takes care of that problem and gives you two or three candleholders at the same time.

Stain the wood with a diluted wood stain if you like. Because you're using treated decking lumber, these can be used outdoors as well as indoors.

Candles in Unexpected Places

On the dinner table…on the mantel…on a birthday cake. Those are the obvious answers to where you place candles. But where else can you use them?

Candlelight is always welcome in unexpected places. This impromptu lantern (it's a plastic trash can in real life) serves two purposes: first, to illuminate a pathway into a dimly lit room, and second, to create an intriguing interplay of light and shape reflected on the ceramic floor.

Candles are a nice bedside touch, whether they're in your room or the guest room. Simple touches added to the holder—strands of beads, a pile of foreign coins, or smooth pebbles—make the arrangement personal and appealing. Pleasantly scented, unlit candles can make drifting off to sleep a pleasure. If you light that bedside candle, be sure that you (or yours) blow it out before you drift off to sleep!

44

A single candle, casually wrapped with an oriental
paper, is paired with an elegant arching branch. A few
rounded pebbles are added to unify the composition,
creating a calming, zen-like arrangement to contemplate
as you soak away the tensions of the day.

The pale green of these tapered
pillars complements the bathroom's color scheme and is
the perfect foil for the stark white tiles. A simple white
saucer and an antique, glass candy dish are inspired candleholder choices.

These plain, cylindrical
candleholders cried out for a
touch of color. We created vases
using tiny glass tea light holders
underneath each cylinder. The
vibrant, summery colors of zinnias
contrast nicely with the rattan
tabletop. Pick a tiny bunch of
violets for spring; use camellias
or galax leaves in the winter.
Or, choose a fragrant flower like a
gardenia and use gardenia-scented
candles to make a strong visual as
well as aromatic statement.

A large, tropical leaf makes an effective mat to
place underneath a simple gathering of tiny ball
candles. It echoes the shape of the container, and
the bold stripes and smooth surface complement
the sheen of the metal.

The hearth of a small fireplace is an inviting setting for a group of candles. The natural seed pods, winding around the arrangement, echo the form of the pear-shape candles. Although three different candles are featured, they share the same color, which unifies the display. The green bowl and plate enhance the overall natural style of this grouping.

If you dream of a white candle, you will soon meet your true love.

Cleaning Up WAX

Table coverings and wood surfaces (including floors) are likely targets for wax spills. Candles will sputter and accidents will happen. Here are three simple remedies for cleaning up wax stains on surfaces.

To remove wax from washable fabrics, gently scrape off as much wax as possible with a dull knife or credit card. Slip a brown paper bag, paper towel, or paper napkin under and on top of the wax stain. Press the papers with a warm iron. The iron will melt the wax onto the paper. Replace the paper with new paper as it becomes saturated with melted wax. Then wash the fabric in warm, sudsy water.

When wax drips onto a wood table your instinct is to wipe it up immediately. Stop! You want to quickly harden the wax, rather than spread it around. Place ice cubes in a plastic bag and hold the ice against the wax to freeze it. Then gently scrape the wax off the wood surface with the back of a table knife or credit card.

If wax drips onto ceramic tiles, use a credit card or craft stick to scrape off the wax. Or, (now don't be afraid!) use a long-tipped lighter to liquify the wax and quickly wipe it up with an absorbent paper towel. You won't hurt the tiles; they've been fired at a much higher temperature than the lighter's flame.

Seasons & Celebrations

A celebration without candles is, well, it just doesn't seem like a celebration. Whether you're enjoying another birthday (how many candles will you need for your next one?), marking the arrival of the winter solstice, or acknowledging the bounty of the harvest, candles are important components and symbols of celebrations around the world.

A thoroughly adult version of the traditional birthday cake, this beauty is perfect for "congratulations on your promotion" and "happy anniversary." Whether you bake it or purchase a store-bought cake on the fly, the addition of simple, thin tapers shout: Celebrate!

Celebrate your favorite fireman's birthday with a four-alarm candle arrangement. Keep the candles lit after the ones on the birthday cake are extinguished. This display will delight a child or remind an adult of a childhood treasure.

Winter

Winter celebrations—especially Christmas and New Year's—are closely linked to the traditions of ancient, pagan midwinter solstice pageants when celebrants lit fires to defy the darkness of winter's first night.

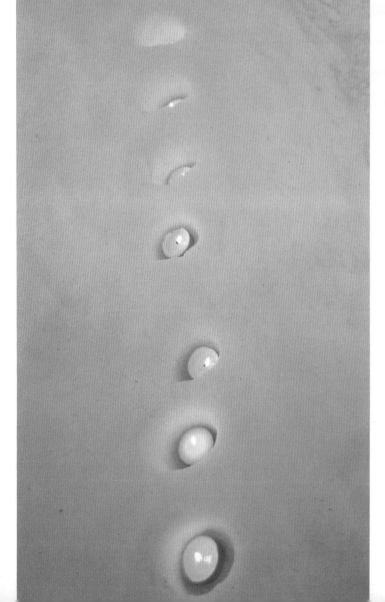

After an inviting blanket of snow has fallen, greet your guests with votives placed in small hollows in the snow. For best results, lightly spray the hollows with water and allow them to freeze before positioning and lighting the candles. The warm glow assures you and your guests that spring will one day return.

Large masses of poinsettias are made even more extravagant with the golden radiance of candles. (Their placement on the stairs is also a not-so-subtle suggestion that guests should stay downstairs.)

This striking, rustic candleholder is not difficult to make.

First, find a shapely fallen tree branch or stick—papery white birch, oak covered in lichen, or perhaps even bamboo. Use a drill to make evenly spaced starter holes along the branch. A sharp pocketknife and rough carving will enlarge the holes to tea light size. If you have access to power-bore or spade bits, you can quickly drill a line of holes large enough for tea lights.

A large and shallow glass container was the inspiration for this arrangement. Welcome the New Year with glass and silver balls that reflect the flicker of candlelight.

Deep red, gold, and the glossy green of holly are
traditional staples of winter holiday decorating. Instead
of placing a red taper in the ubiquitous brass candlestick,
mass red votives in a metal serving tray. You can move
the light to wherever you need it.

Mexican tinwork is highly collectible. If you happen upon a multi-branched candelabra snap it up. Adorned with feathery "leaves," it makes a stunning addition to any holiday decor.

In Germany, the fragrant evergreen tree was traditionally adorned with tiny white candles that were lit on Christmas Eve. Today, candles on trees are battery or electrically powered, but the symbol of the lighted candle remains an important part of the holiday.

This stunning candlescape is a transitional arrangement that showcases the russet hues of autumn and the serene pallor of winter. The wheat-colored pillars complement the natural materials, while the white candles point toward a season of frosty, star-bright winter nights.

If you accidentally knock over a candle, there will be a wedding soon.

Celebrations Around the World

DIWALI

The festival of Diwali marks the beginning of the new year for Hindus. The festival takes place over an entire week during October or November, with the biggest celebration on the night of the new moon. Traditionally, small oil lamps called diyas are lit and placed everywhere. In urban areas, candles are used for the diyas. These lamps welcome the spirits of the dead home.

In northern India, Diwali is a celebration of Rama's triumphant homecoming after his 14-year exile. Rama is the seventh reincarnation of the Lord Vishnu, and the embodiment of truth and morality. The candles of Diwali represent the spiritual illumination that Rama's return brings.

In Gujurat, the western-most state of India, the festival of Diwali honors Lakshmi, the goddess of spiritual and material wealth. Lakshmi is also the divine consort of Lord Vishnu. As people believe that she will not enter a dark house, they light many diyas to tempt her into stopping and blessing their homes.

El DIA de los MUERTOS

The Day of the Dead—a blend of the Catholic All Saint's Day and an indigenous Zapotec Indian celebration—is celebrated in graveyards all over Mexico on October 31. During the day, simulated funeral processions wind through villages. Sugar skulls, bright paper flowers and marigolds, treats for the departed, and candles are brought to the cemetery to adorn family plots. As midnight approaches, the candles are lit on each grave and incense perfumes the air. The atmosphere of the holiday is both solemn and celebratory.

HANUKKAH

The eight-day Jewish celebration of Hanukkah, The Festival of Lights, commemorates the victory of the Maccabees against the vast Greek armies that besieged Jerusalem. Because of the battles, the Jews were unable to celebrate the harvest festival of Succot. After the Greeks were sent packing, the Jews celebrated Succot while they rebuilt and rededicated the desecrated Temple.

The *menorah*, a candleholder for nine candles, is an important symbol of the celebration. The candleholder must have eight candles placed at the same height; the ninth candle, the shamesh, is raised above them. One candle is lit with the shamesh on the first night, two on the second, and so on until all are lit on the eighth night.

KWANZA

The African-American community celebrates this holiday from December 26 to January 1. A holiday of recent lineage, it was created in 1966 by Maulana Karenga, a professor at California State University. Kwanza celebrates seven principles: unity, self-determination, collective work and responsibility, cooperative economics, purpose, creativity, and faith.

The *kinara*, an important symbol of the holiday, represents respect for African ancestors and holds seven candles which symbolize the seven principles: three red, three green, and one black. Each night during the week-long holiday one candle is lit to symbolize the giving of light and life to the principle celebrated that day.

LOI KRATHONG

Once the sun has set and the full moon of mid-November begins to cast its milky glow over the fields of Thailand, the country's rivers and waterways come alive with lights of their own. Fleets of small boats, fashioned from banana leaves or paper, are set afloat on rivers and waterways. Lighted candles, flowers, coins, and sweetly scented incense fill the little boats under the light of the full moon.

The tradition began when one of King Ramakhamhaeng's wives devised a way to please him and Lord Buddha simultaneously. She created a paper lantern that resembled a lotus flower, the symbol of the human spirit, and set it afloat on the river bearing a lighted candle. The king was so delighted by this act that he ordered all subjects to perform similar boat launches on a designated night every year.

60

Autumn Holidays

Harvest festivals are celebrated around the world (usually, but not always, in autumn).

Artfully carved squash and turnips—carved in the same manner as the traditional jack-o'-lantern—are almost too pretty to be placed on the doorstep to greet trick-or-treaters. The graphic designs appeal more to adult tastes than the traditional, but far from stodgy, Halloween ghosts and goblins.

An antique, bronze Nataraj—
the dancing form of Lord
Shiva—presides over this casual,
late-summer array of bright
marigolds and candles.

With few exceptions, most candleholders can be used indoors and out.
This artfully rusted sconce looks
equally at home on the living room
wall as it does outdoors (page 86).
Wire silk autumn leaves and composition berries onto a plain candleholder
for a more sophisticated and
celebratory look.

Elegant shapes and oversize, gilded acorns make this mantel arrangement a showstopping seasonal decoration. The cinnamon-scented candles add just the right touch of autumnal aroma to the air.

This "haunted" house is cheery and welcoming. The brightly striped squashes are a refreshing change from the traditional carved pumpkin. When you tire of them, slice them in half, and pop them into the oven to bake.

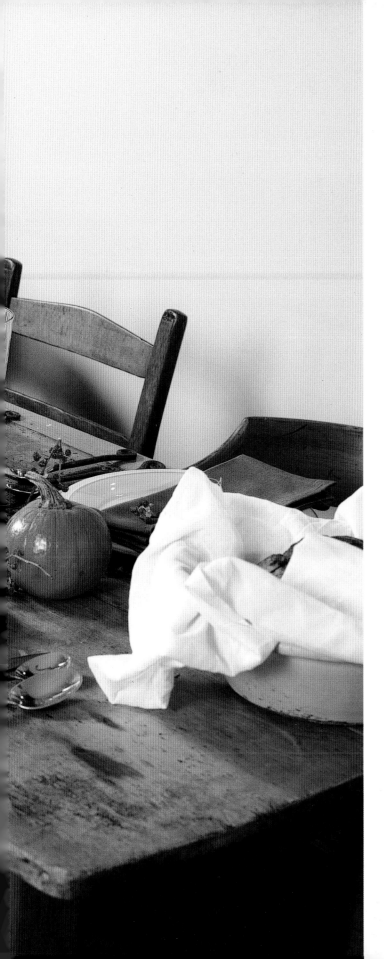

Large glass vases filled with pecans and chestnuts make attractive candleholders for a rustic, autumn table setting. A bit of candle adhesive on the bottom of the taper will hold it in place while you place the nuts in the vase. Twining yellow and red strands of bittersweet vine with accents of small, shiny pumpkins is an easy way to celebrate the season's glorious colors. The arrangement is casually comfortable, perfect for a dinner with close friends. Polished pebbles, glass marbles, or strands of pearls could be used in vases to create different tablescape themes.

67

Spring & Summer

The warmth of summer beckons us outdoors, but there's no reason you can't bring the beauty of outdoors into your home.

Nestle pale summer flowers in a cairn of smoothly burnished stones from the shore. Tea lights, small pillars, and touches of faux pearls simply add to the glamour of this candlescape.

First, build your cairn down the center of the dinner table, along the mantle or on a sideboard. Tuck tea lights and small pillars at intervals among the stones. Sturdy flowers like white chrysanthemums can survive an evening without water, so just tuck them in at the last minute. The faux pearls can be found in the floral and bridal aisles of most craft stores.

not create simple candle arrangements while you're on vacation?
ll make the beachside cottage as appealing as your own home. Gather
shells and stones on your beach stroll, then combine them with things
around the cottage. Here, someone saved a few rusty graters,
em linger in the salt air, and gave them new life as quirky lanterns.

Eggs—the universal symbol of fertility and growth—are a common springtime symbol, especially around the Easter holidays. Europeans and Americans alike use and decorate them in many ways. Small, egg-shape candles are nestled in beds of live grass. If you can't find egg-shape candles, make small container candles (page 9) in blown egg shells.

Cool as spring, pale green cake plates are stacked atop each other to present delicate, delicious-looking pastries. The top one holds small votives lending a festive air to the event. We tried placing candles on all three tiers, but the properties of heat convection (it rises, you know) resulted in a waxy mass on the top plate. Be forewarned.

Candles Outdoors

Candlelight in the garden...is there anything more lovely? Have a seat. Linger in the cool green. Breath deeply. Enjoy the designs created on the foliage by the flickering light. Relax.

A collection of lanterns—hung on shepherd's crook plant hangers, placed on the stone wall, and nestled in the greenery—provides lambent light in this outdoor room.

Placing lit candles on an outdoor side table creates an inviting, festive, and useful glow for a party. How else will your guests find a flat surface upon which to set appetizers and drinks? The glass tabletop reflects the flickering flames. A curved stove grating—a lucky, but not uncommon find from a scrap-metal yard—makes a great arabesque screen.

LIGHTING Candles

Refrigerated candles (especially tapers) burn more evenly and slowly.

Before your guests arrive, light and extinguish the candles. When you light them again, they'll light quickly and burn evenly.

Light a candle with a lit candle. If you have many candles to light, this saves you from striking match after match and the irritation of singed fingertips.

The long-tipped butane lighters used for igniting outdoor grills make candle lighting a breeze.

At the dinner table, light the candles just before everyone is seated. Allow them to burn until everyone has left the table.

Using Candles OUTDOORS

Don't leave uncovered candles out overnight. Moisture will be drawn into the wick and the candle may not relight. Another danger is that water will actually become trapped underneath the wax. If the candle is lit, the trapped water will heat up and eventually explode, splattering hot wax everywhere.

When burning candles outside, always pay attention to which way the wind is blowing. Keep the candle flame shielded so that it burns evenly, and keep the candle far from flammable objects such as overhanging branches and surrounding foliage. And never ever leave a candle burning unattended.

A candle in the wind? Yes, a flickering flame is lovely, but we all know the truth: Unless you protect your flame it sputters out unattractively. Use traditional hurricane shades if you have them. Or, press other glass objects into use—vases, light-fixture shades, lab glass, and jars. Yes, the black wire basket makes a striking candleholder, but the first gentle breeze will snuff the flame.

For sheer drama this candle display is hard to beat. If you've saved those vases from past flower arrangements, you have it made. If no one sends you flowers anymore, purchase inexpensive vases from second-hand stores. Mix colors, textures, and sizes. The reflections on the glass tabletop are a bonus.

On the night of the new moon, light a green candle and money will come to you. (Don't light the candle from a fire though, or you will never be prosperous.)

Happy little lanterns made from tin cans and tea lights—what could be simpler?

Fill clean cans with water and pop them in the freezer overnight. Use a sharp awl to pierce holes in each can. The frozen water prevents the can from collapsing as you press the awl through the metal. Run hot water over the can and remove the ice. Cut a short length of wire to use as a hanger.

Even tin cans unadorned with snappy colors and graphics can be used to create innovative container candles. Remove the paper labels and wire rims of tin cans in a variety of sizes. Cut out triangles along the top edge with tin snips. Curl each triangle that remains by rolling it around a small dowel or pencil. Place a weighted wick in each can and fill it with wax. Scent the wax with an insect repellent like citronella if you wish to use the candles outdoors.

Lead guests to your door or down the garden path with a variety of glowing orchid pots lining the walkway.

A **silver salver** laden with votives will make your garden glow. Solder a copper pipe coupler to the bottom of a silver plated tray. Insert a length of copper pipe into the coupler and solder it as well. Viola! Light is served.

A terra-cotta planter filled with white gravel is a versatile outdoor candleholder. Scatter decorative stones around the metal tea light holders and pair the arrangement with a potted succulent. A gathering of small, glass votive holders could be nestled on the stones as well.

Extinguishing CANDLES

Hold your finger in front of the candle flame and blow at it. The air will flow around the finger, extinguish the candle evenly, and prevent hot wax from spattering.

Use a long-handled candle snuffer or douter to put out tapers. Its small, conical shape fits over the candle flame and extinguishes it.

Cup your hand behind the flame when you blow out a candle. Doing so prevents hot wax from splattering on your furniture or linens.

A trick for extinguishing tapers for the brave and nimble fingered who don't wish to blow: Moisten the tips of your thumb and forefinger, then deftly pinch the wick.

This rusted iron candle sconce looks as handsome outdoors as it did indoors (page 63). Purchase a pair of light shades from the home improvement store and use them as hurricane shades when you take a candleholder outdoors.

What could be lovelier than the flicker of tiny flames reflected in dark water? Floating candles have been placed in this water feature (it was once a deep, stone sink) for a special occasion. Place the candles sparingly in the water to avoid singeing the water plants.

If you don't have a permanent water feature in your garden, create this delightful temporary one. Galvanized buckets, tubs, and basins are stacked, arranged, and filled with water. And those aren't water lilies glowing in the water!

A pair of lanterns illuminates the bright flowers planted next to this bench. The light creates a romantic mood and draws attention to the hot colors in the gathering dusk.

Imagine a bevy of these leafy lanterns illuminating your midsummer's night eve. They're oh-so-simple to create.

Gather a few fresh leaves or use dried and pressed leaves. Retrieve clean glass jars from your recycling bin. Trim lengths of translucent paper with decorative-edge scissors to wrap around each jar. Cut generous lengths of twine, and use each piece to secure a leaf and a length of paper around the jar. Cut four lengths of wire for each jar, and twist each wire securely around the rim of the jar to make a hanger. Place a votive candle or tea light in each lantern to silhouette the delicate tracery of each leaf's structure.

These linen bags are a twist on paper bag luminarias, but the principle is the same. Fill the bags with sand to weight them. Then place tea lights or votive candles in glass holders inside the bags. They'll also look great indoors.

Don't forget: The glow of candles indoors looks just as lovely when seen from the outside. Invite your guests in with the beauty of shimmering lights. When they leave, that last glimpse of the evening's candlelight will linger in their memories all the way home.

Special Photography

Index